Public Speaking 101

Public Speaking Guide for Beginners

TABLE OF CONTENTS

Introduction 1

Chapter 1: Getting Started 2

Chapter 2: Overcome Your Fear 5

Chapter 3: Delivering Your Speech 13

Chapter 4: The Speaker and the Audience 20

Chapter 5: Getting Deeper In the Parts of Your Speech 24

Chapter 6: Proper Use of Language 30

Chapter 7: Speech Delivery 32

Conclusion.. 38

INTRODUCTION

I want to thank you and congratulate you for downloading the book, *"Public Speaking 101: Public Speaking Guide for Beginners"*.

This book contains proven steps and strategies on how to start public speaking as a beginner.

This book will help you get started and provide you with the basic information you need to start public speaking.

This book also contains steps on how to overcome your fear of public speaking, and other important information you need to know about delivering a public speech.

Thanks again for downloading this book, I hope you enjoy it!

CHAPTER 1

Getting Started

What is Public Speaking?

Public speaking is a form of communication in which a speaker delivers a message to a certain group of people or an audience.

The speaker communicates with his or her audience with a specific purpose in mind. Public speaking mainly involves a speaker, an audience and a message. It can take place anywhere and can be done by anyone.

You see people ever day transmit messages to maybe dozens or even hundreds of people.

It happens in your workplace, in school and in your own community. It can be done by many people including lecturers, businessmen, bosses and managers.

Not many people are comfortable with the thought of public speaking. That is why not so many people are good at it. But if you become a good public speaker, you will come to realize that it can give you a lot of advantages.

Having the ability to talk in front of many people and convince them gives you some sort of authority and power.

If you become a good public speaker, you will be able to deliver great speeches and move a whole crowd.

You will be able to speak anywhere, anytime comfortably. You can deliver your message in a classroom across dozens of students or even in your workplace with hundreds of employees. You will be able to make the most out of every situation.

Reasons Why You Should Learn Public Speaking...

There are specific careers where you are expected to have good communication skills. Sometimes, it is a part of an individual's job to talk and convince people.

If you are a lawyer, a politician, a pastor, a sales representative or a journalist, this skill is a must-have for you.

However, the truth is, good communication skills are a must-have for everybody.

In the real world, you cannot go through your day without communicating.

Sooner or later, you'll have to talk to your boss, your coworkers, and even to strangers. Here are a few more reasons why you should learn public speaking...

1. It is a skill that will help you succeed in life
   Most employers look for good communication skills when it comes to new employees.
   The ability to communicate well through oral and written means is sometimes more important than having raw knowledge.
   With good communication skills, you will be able to relate well with other employees and when given a group project, you can easily build up teamwork with each other.
   Having the ability to speak well in public will give you a boost when it comes to work.
   It will help you greatly in maintaining good relationships with your co-workers and have great career development.
   Having good communications skills will also help you in your personal life. You will be able to meet and talk to more people and increase your opportunities in life.
2. You will be able to learn practical and useful skills
   Public speaking will develop you as a person and as a professional. Your ability to think and reason will be sharpened as you study public speaking.

As you practice making your speeches, you will learn how to construct meaningful sentences and whole paragraphs that properly convey the message you want to be delivered.

These skills that you will learn will benefit you not only when you do public speaking but also through your career and life.

You can use these skills anywhere and anytime you need them.

3. You will be able to mingle comfortably with people whoever they may be

Public speaking prepares you to speak in front of an audience.

This "audience" is not a definite group of people. It may consist of men, and woman, young and old, coming from different places all over the world.

With public speaking, you will learn to talk to different people from different walks of life.

This will allow you to respect different points of view from people belonging to different cultures, genders and ages.

It will also help you bring yourself closer to your audience and you will be able to make a stable connection between yourself and the people whom you are talking to.

CHAPTER 2

Overcome Your Fear

Overcoming Your Fear of Public Speaking

Most people are afraid of public speaking.

Although you may not know this, being afraid of speaking can be a source of many setbacks in your career.

Nervousness is a natural thing to feel when you are about to speak in front of many people. If you don't have much knowledge and experience about what you are doing you will really feel anxious about doing it.

You may think that your nervousness will only bring you failure.

After all you can't do anything right if you are jittery. But if you learn how to use it properly your nervousness might in fact give you an advantage.

1. Identify the Source

    Identifying the source of your fear may be hard. Sometimes, you just don't know why you feel afraid.

    But sometimes, you just don't want to accept it. Learning to face and acknowledge the source of your fear will help you when you start public speaking.

    You will become more aware of what makes you anxious and you can take definite steps to ease yourself.

    o Negative Experiences

Negative experiences naturally cause trauma. A speech you did may have had an unpleasant outcome.

People may have laughed at you or maybe they did not listen. These negative experiences make you feel bad about yourself and about what you did.

It has different effects to different people. Some may see it as a challenge that they need to overcome.

Others see it as a sign that they are not good at what they are doing and that they need to stop.

o   Being the Center of Attention

There are people who just love being the center of attention, but there are also people who hate it.

They dread feeling that everyone is looking at them and seeing every movement they do.

The fact that everyone will see them make a single mistake is somehow terrifying to them to the point that they avoid being the center of attention at all cost.

o   Being New And Inexperienced

New speakers always tend to be anxious. Sometimes, because of their lack of experience, they feel that they are doing everything wrong.

They think that they are alone in front of many people without anyone ever paying attention.

They feel different or apart from their audience and they start to panic.

Am I doing it right? Is anyone really paying attention? Do I look okay? Questions keep flooding their minds until they feel more and more anxious and start to lose focus on what they are doing.

2.   Identify the Exact Situation When Nervousness Strikes

- o Nervousness can come to different people at different times. Some may feel nervous at the beginning of a speech before even starting and then they become alright as soon as the speech starts.
- o Some may feel fine at first but feel anxious as the speech progresses. Some may be fine while delivering the whole speech but later on be anxious about audience feedback.
- o As pinpointing the source of your fear, it is also important to know when fear strikes you. It will help you be better prepared for the things that might happen and keep calm while speaking.

3. Ensure Success Through Boosting Your Confidence

Here are a few things that you need to do before your speech:

- o Prepare Well

  The preparation process is just as important as the actual speech. In fact, sometimes, preparation is more important than the speech itself.

  Without proper preparation, you will lose confidence and be unsure of what to do and what not to do.

  Preparation gives you the mindset that you are going to speak in front of a large number of people. This will help you be calmer and focused when you do the actual thing.

- o Practice

  Practice makes perfect. Everybody knows that, but only a few people take this idea seriously. Like preparation, practice is sometimes more important to focus on that the real speech.

  If you are a warrior going to a battle, sharpening your sword and honing your skills is more important that the battle itself.

After all, if you go to battle with a rusty blade, you'll die in an instant. You can't just sit there and wait for things to happen. You need to make thing happen.

Here is a way to practice your speech:

After making your speech, stand in front of a mirror. Before even saying anything, check your posture. Are you standing straight? Are you smiling? Do you look nervous?

Be sure to have proper posture and a smile in your face. Then take a minute or two to close your eyes and imagine the surroundings. How many people are there? Is the place big? Are you comfortable?

Take it all in and try to relax. Open your eyes, still imagining your surroundings, and start your speech.

Pay close attention to what you say and how you say it. Look at how you stand and how you address your "audience".

You can take a video of yourself speaking if you want to. And then review it afterwards.

You can also ask your friends to watch you give your speech and then ask for what they think needs to be improved.

○ Have a Positive Mental Attitude

Before making your speech, you should have a positive attitude. Avoid any negative thoughts and think only of the good things that will happen.

Your mind is a powerful tool that you can use to achieve success. What you think, you will believe. So think about the good things and hope for the best. Your mental attitude is important when it comes down to the actual speech.

Tell yourself that you can do it, and you will succeed. Tell yourself otherwise, and you will fail.

Believe in what you can do and try your best to not lose your focus.

o   Envision the Success You Want

You may be familiar with visualization. It is when you visualize or think of things happening even before they happen or maybe just because you want to imagine them.

Maybe you don't do this anymore thinking that it's kid stuff, but what you don't know, is you can use this to give yourself an advantage.

Many people visualize the success they want and often, what they imagine comes true.

That is the power of your mind. Visualizing success is connected with thinking positively.

When you think positively while visualizing success, you will give yourself greater chances to do better things…

Start by finding a quiet place. Sit down and close your eyes. Don't do this in your bed, since you may fall asleep.

Get comfortable with your chair, your surroundings, and the sound of silence around you. Start to visualize the start of the day when you are going to give your speech.

You get up from your bed, full of energy and confidence. You put on your clothes.

You look good and feel good about yourself. You leave the house with a smile on your face and you drive to the place where you will be delivering your speech.

As you arrive, you greet people and they comment on how good you look for the day.

You exchange warm smiles and handshakes. You are prepared and excited for your speech. Then as you start talking, you see yourself comfortably interacting with the people around you.

They laugh and smile and pay attention to what you are saying. As your speech finishes, people give a round of applause and you receive good feedback from your audience.

That is how you can visualize your success. Of course, the concept of success is different for every individual.

You can make a few changes and add a few more positive feelings.

Make things work for you just the way you want them to. The details are purely up to you and your imagination so be creative.

Try doing this every once in a while and you will see yourself becoming more successful and confident.

4. Take A Moment to Relax and Take a Break
   o Meditate

   Find a quiet place or corner to sit down and meditate. Close your eyes if you think it will help you.

   Focus on trying to relax your muscles and keeping your breathing pattern normal.

   Do this for ten to twenty minutes until you feel more calm and relaxed.

   o Do Breathing Exercises

   Inhale air as much as you can and then breath is all out. Try to create your own breathing pattern.

As you get more comfortable with your breathing, try to tell yourself something that will help soothe you.

You can use words like "calm" or "relax" or you can use your own mantra.

Say these words as you exhale and try to focus on your own thoughts as you inhale. Remember to keep a positive attitude and follow your mantra.

Do this breathing exercise once every day before your scheduled speech to get your mind set on what you are about to do. Also try to do this exercise right before delivering your speech.

5. Make Your Movements Matter

Making movements when delivering a speech is not just used to persuade your audience or show conviction. It can be also used as channel to let out your fear in a more positive manner.

You can release your tension through the small movements you make with your body. Just standing there in front of many people is just plain boring. And it also shows how tense you are. Make movements while you are speaking. It's just like having a conversation with your friends. Don't act everything out. It doesn't need to be scripted.

Try to be normal and convincing. Also try to move from one place to another from time to time.

Making movements, no matter how small they are, will help you to release the pressure that you are feeling. In addition to that, it will also help you keep your audience's attention.

6. Ask for Feedback

After delivering your speech, asking for your audience feedback is important. Although you may not like what some people will tell you, it is a way of helping yourself improve.

Of course you cannot always tell if you are doing the right thing. From your perspective, what you did may have been perfect.

However, if you try to look at things from a different point of view, things might be a little off. Sometimes, you just can't pinpoint the things that you are doing wrong.

You still can evaluate your own performance, but hearing other people's opinions is a lot better.

Be it good or bad, audience feedback will help you improve as a speaker. It will help you do better next time and avoid the errors that you have already made.

CHAPTER 3

Delivering Your Speech

Steps to Delivering a Public Speech:

1. Select Your Topic

    Before even starting making a draft for your speech, you first need to select a topic.

    You can't just dive in and write down all sorts of stuff. Decide on what you want to talk about – a specific topic you want to address.

    There are many different types of speeches and you can talk about many different things. You inspire change in your audience and motivate them. You can move them to tears or bring them to laughter.

    You can make speeches in weddings, birthdays, anniversaries, in your workplace and even in your own home, among your family members. If you were assigned to make a speech for a certain occasion then prepare your speech for that specific reason.

    If however, you not bound by these limits, then you can pick out anything – anything at all – and talk about it.

    Of course it would be an advantage if you are, to some extent, familiar with your topic.

    This will allow you to talk and deliver you speech with ease. However, if trying new things seems challenging, then just go ahead and do it.

But as you select your topic, you should also think about the interests your audience too.

2. Know Your Audience

   After selecting your topic, the next thing to do is to know your audience.

   Your audience may have different personalities, likes and dislikes, and have different opinions on certain subjects.

   They may come from different races, genders and age groups. As a speaker, you need to acknowledge this diversity and learn to accept it.

   Take into consideration the factors among your audience that can affect how they will perceive your chosen or given topic.

3. Know Your Purpose

   Next, decide on what you want to do in your speech. What do you want your audience to feel or do after listening to you?

   There are three general purposes of a speech: to persuade, inform and celebrate a special occasion.

   o Inform

      An informative speech gives the audience new and valuable information. It gives its audience a different perspective to a given subject.

      It increases the audience's awareness and knowledge by learning new information. Informative speeches may include social media, sexuality and climate change.

   o Persuade

A persuasive speech aims to convince an audience. It attempts to persuade the audience to change their beliefs, values and attitudes.

This type of speech may be hard to do as novice speaker.

You need to have good foundation and a good source of information that will support your claims and eventually make your audience believe you.

o   Celebrate a Special Occasion

Speeches are commonly done in celebrating special occasions.

These occasions may include weddings, funerals, birthdays, graduations, anniversaries, commencements and many more.

Speeches done during special occasions often tend to inspire, entertain and of course, celebrate.

A speech done during special occasions can be informative, persuasive, or a mix of both.

4.   Define Your Main Points.

Your speech should not go around just mentioning things here and there.

You can't just randomly tell something and then go back to the topic once you notice that your audience is already bored.

To avoid losing your focus on your topic, your speech should have at least two to three main points. You will focus on these main points while delivering your speech. If it is an informative speech, then your main points must be the main thoughts and ideas that you want to impart to your audience.

If it is a persuasive speech, the main points must be the vital arguments that you want to present.

Write these main points down in order and keep it in mind. It will help you maintain concentration on the topics that you want to discuss.

5. Divide Your Speech Into Parts

Ever since elementary, you have been taught that an essay mainly has three parts – the introduction, body and conclusion.

These three parts are crucial when doing a speech for each of them has a purpose to serve.

o   Introduction

The introduction's main purpose is to open the speech and introduce it to the audience.

This is also the part where the speaker introduces himself or herself. You should "hook" your audience's attention to you using the introduction.

If it turns out good, your audience will listen to you. However, if it turns out bad, your audience will get bored and not pay attention.

You can catch your audience's attention by a saying a phrase, a quote, a story or even a bible verse.

After getting their attention, you introduce the topic and tell them the purpose of your speech. (Answer the questions "What?" and "Why?")

Tell the audience what are main ideas that you will share with them. Then slowly move towards the body of your speech.

o   Body

The body contains the speech's main points. This is the main part of your speech. It is where the research and most of information comes in.

- ○ Conclusion

  In this part, you do a review of what you did. Recall the main ideas and arguments you have presented.

  This is also the question-and-answer portion of your speech. This is the part where you let your audience talk and ask you some questions.

  You can also ask the audience your questions and see if they have learned something from you.

  And finally, leave your audience with something to ponder on for the rest of the day.

6. Make An Outline

Professional speakers do not need to look at papers when they speak. That's what makes them professional.

They know what exactly they are talking about and do not need any reference when they talk about it. They know their speech by heart and can talk about it without much thinking.

However, as a beginner with not much experience, you need some sort of guide to help you get across the different points of your speech.

Making an outline not only helps you to determine the important points of your speech but also to memorize it.

You can select from different organizational patterns to arrange your speech. You can just use bullets and numbers for a simple outline.

However, if you want something more detailed, you can use coordinate and subordinate points.

Examples:

Bullets:

- Point #1
- Point #2
- Point #3

Numbering:

1. Fact #1
2. Fact #2
3. Fact #3

Coordinate Points:

1. Main Argument #1
2. Main Argument #2

Subordinate Points:

1. Main Argument #1
   A. Main Support #1
     1. Idea #1
     2. Idea #2
       a. Statement #1
       b. Statement #2

The outline of your speech will be up to you and your speech's contents.

You can choose any style you want as long as you arrange them into a neat order. Use this outline as a guide during your speech.

7. Prepare Your Aids

Presentation aids help you help you through the discussion of your speech and in getting the attention of your audience.

They also help the audience retain information and helps you show emphasis to a point. You can prepare a presentation with graphs, charts, images and videos as long as it is connected to your speech.

Informative speeches need graphic aids to impart more information while persuasive speeches need it to better convince people.

You can use your presentation aids to summarize and highlight important information. It can also be used to explain different theories and complex ideas.

It will no doubt help you and your audience to understand each other better.

8. Practice

Here are a few things that you need to keep in mind while practicing your speech:

- o Do not speak in monotone
- o Pay attention to the rate of how you speak
- o Practice your pronunciation
- o Pay attention to the loudness of your voice
- o Practice your phrasing
- o Smile
- o Practice your gestures
- o Make eye contact
- o React to what you are saying

CHAPTER 4

The Speaker and the Audience

Selective Listening

Even though you are saying the exact same words to two different people, sometimes, they will not perceive your message in a similar manner.

The other one might pay good attention to you and totally understand what you are saying.

In addition, the other one might just ignore you and have no exact idea of what you are talking about.

It is because people listen and pay attention to things selectively.

People only seem to pay attention to what they think is important and to what they can relate to based on their experiences.

In other words, someone might pay attention to you if you two find some common ground.

As a speaker, you need to get the attention of as much people as possible. You can do this by:

1. Identifying in advance what is important to your audience. This may include their interests, values and beliefs.
2. Show them what they can get by listening to you. What are the benefits that you can give them?
3. Try to relate to them by telling your own experiences. You may have had the same experience with an audience. Or you may have felt the same way under the same situations.
4. Repeat important and meaningful ideas in your speech and give them emphasis. However, don't say the same phrase

again and again. Try to tell it to your audience in a different way.

5. Use presentation aids to highlight your message and keep your audience's attention.

How to Deal With Distractions:

A part of speaking includes common distractions and as a speaker, you need to know how to deal with them.

Chatting is a common distraction found in any social event. When someone is speaking, you expect everyone to listen.

There will always be people who will chat with each while you speak in front.

The proper respond to this is to look at the persons talking and pause until they notice you and stop.

When they stop, smile and continue from where you left off. You should give sudden distractions like phone calls minimal response and proceed with your speech.

The more you give it attention, the more you allow you and your audience to lose focus. So keep going and try to disregard the noise if it doesn't need attention.

If an audience interrupts you in the middle of your speech and asks you a question, keep it in mind and get back to it at the end of your speech.

Know How Your Listeners Feel Towards the Given Topic

Different people may have different reactions or opinions towards a topic.

At the beginning of your speech, you should try to know how much your audience knows about the matter you are talking about.

Determine if they have a positive, negative or neutral attitude towards your topic. Once you have this information, make progress with the speech accordingly.

If the topic is new to listeners, you should start slow and build progress from there.

Your listeners do not have much knowledge and information about the topic so it may take them some time to take in all the information.

You can tell your audience the relevance of the topic in their personal lives to make them listen and pay attention.

You can also relate the topic to familiar ideas to see if they will react positively or negatively.

If your audience knows little about your topic, stick to details that are easy to comprehend and provide background or supporting details.

Immediately define terms that may be new or confusing to your audience and don't sue too much words.

Keep your sentences short, simple and comprehensible.

Do not use unnecessary words. It will only confuse your audience and will not make your speech any better.

Also try to repeat important ideas and at the end, try to condense huge chunks of information into tiny bits of clear and logical ideas.

Analyze Your Audience

When talking to a large crowd, you can't exactly know if the people are listening to what you are saying and accepting your ideas.

Someone may be looking at you while you deliver your speech from start to finish, but in reality, that someone may have the faintest idea of what you have been talking about.

Some might appear to agree with your thoughts but in reality he or she is actually thinking about something else.

On the other hand, someone might not look at you as you deliver you speech but he or she understood every single word that you said. It is easy for many people to lie about their thoughts and feelings.

As a speaker, you need to see through these lies and be able to tell whether someone is paying attention or not.

Although you cannot ask people outright if they are truly listening to what you are saying, you can actually look for these signs in their body language.

If someone is interested in what you are saying, he or she will smile and maintain eye contact with you.

This means that he or she is open to your ideas and somehow takes a liking to you. If someone does otherwise, it may mean that he or she is not interested in what you are saying.

A frown and an averted glance usually shows disagreement or lack of interest.

You can also tell if a person is open for communication by looking at his arms or hands. If someone's arms are crossed across his or her chest, it may mean that he or she does not want to talk to you.

This type of body language is called "closed body language". The person tries to protect himself or create a barrier by folding his or her arms across the chest and avoiding contact. As soon as you notice people losing their focus, try to call on their attention immediately.

Increase audience interaction and try to invite one or two people to speak and tell you what they think.

This will bring back attention and perhaps spark some interest among the audience.

CHAPTER 5

Getting Deeper In the Parts of Your Speech

The Introduction and Conclusion

As the introduction begins your speech, the conclusion ends it.

Many speakers do not pay much attention to these two parts, thinking that if the body of the speech is well constructed, then the introduction and conclusion will just come into the right place.

This type of thinking will lead you to failure. Not only do you not know what to do and say, but you also lack practice and preparation.

A good speaker pays good attention to all the parts of his speech and understands that each is vital to deliver his or her message effectively.

A good introduction opens up the topic to your listeners and prepares them for the main discussion. It's like an appetizer served before the main dish to add suspense and anticipation.

A good introduction needs to attract your audience and keep their attention. You must keep them curious and expectant. The conclusion ends the speech.

In this part, you address your audience's questions and know if they really learned something from you.

The Introduction

The introduction is vital to the outcome of your speech. In this part, your audience will decide whether to listen to you or not. It plays a big part in getting the attention of your listeners.

You introduction must be made after you complete the body of your speech.

By doing this, you will be able to immediately know the contents of the body and do a "preview"accordingly. It must be short and simple.

It should only take about ten to fifteen percent of the whole speech. After making your draft, try to practice it and then make changes later on.

A good introduction must (a) get your listeners' attention and enthusiasm.

It should also (b) open the topic and tell your listeners the main point and ideas you want to tell them.

Lastly, a good introduction must (c) convince your audience that what you are saying is true and well-founded.

Get Your Listeners' Attention and Enthusiasm

You must open your speech with a bang. If you want to get the attention of your listeners, you must do it in the most effective way possible.

Even though you have already a well-formed body, the introduction still must be just as good.

During the introduction, your audience will determine whether you are worth listening to or not. Here are a few ways to jump-start your introduction:

A Quote

A good quotation is one that concisely describes the topic of your speech. This quotation, when used properly will draw the attention of your audience immediately.

Quotations are a good source of knowledge, information and thoughts to ponder. When you get your audience curious and interested, they will surely listen to you.

A Story

When you tell someone a good story, he or she will eventually get hooked and would want to know how the story ends. You can use this technique to catch the attention of your audience.

You can tell them your own personal story or a story from one of your friends.

Just make sure that it relates to your topic. It will just be like sharing an experience with other people.

With that, you can find some common ground, and things might get a little more interesting from there.

Humor

If you do it well, using humor may be a good way to start your speech. Not only will it lighten the mood, but it will also create laughter and a hint of camaraderie with one another.

It will put your audience to ease and will allow you to state your main point while they listen. It can be away to open things up a little bit easier, but remember to use it with caution. Too much humor can lead to lack of attention from your audience. You can't laugh all throughout your speech. Remember that the most important thing is for you to deliver your message properly.

However, making jokes every once in a while may also be good.

If you notice that your audience's attention is not on you anymore, try to tell them one or two jokes to get their focus back.

A Question

A question always sparks curiosity and eventually, you will get the interest of your listeners.

When you ask your audience a question, they will eventually want to hear the answer eventually, or perhaps, there are times when your audience already knows the answer; you just need to give them an idea of what your speech is all about.

There are questions that encourage response and there are also questions that stimulate thinking. By posing an intriguing question, you will get your listeners' attention in no time.

Open the Topic and Tell the Main Points

The introduction is the part where you reveal a little bit of the body. In a way, you give it a "preview".

Many novice speakers forget this important function of the introduction, thinking that they should only focus on getting the audience's attention.

Remember that after getting their attention, you need to tell them what the topics that you will be discussing with them are.

Preview your topic and purpose in a brief and concise sentence. Do not take too long or your audience will get bored. However, do not make it too short or they may not get the idea.

After that, it is the time to tell your audience the main points. You need to tell them the main ideas that you will be discussing with them in order.

Just like the preview, the main points should be brief. You do not need to explain it in detail because that part will be in the body of your speech.

Convince Your Audience

The last function of the introduction is to convince your audience and make them believe you.

You have to motivate the audience to listen to you.

To make this happen, you must persuade your audience that the topic you will be discussing is important and you are capable to discuss it.

Your audience needs to know the importance of your topic immediately. Whether they should or should not pay attention to your speech.

A way to make your audience listen is by telling them what they will be able to gain if they listened to you. How can they apply the things that you will tell them in their daily lives?

Try to answer this question in your introduction and catch their attention immediately.

The Conclusion

Your conclusion is just as important as any part of your speech.

Even though this is the end and you have finished opening the topic (introduction) and completed the main discussion (body), you still have to end your speech.

The main purpose of the conclusion is to tell your audience that the speech is about to end. Just like the introduction, the conclusion is done after the body and it only consists about ten percent of the speech.

The conclusion does not simply end your speech; it should also inspire and motivate your audience.

Here are a few things that you need to do when you end your speech:

Send a Signal and Give Proper Closure

As you approach the end, of the body, you will not just say "thank you" and "goodbye" at the end of your speech.

The conclusion needs some sort of transition to signal the audience that it is the end.

You can say phrases like "finally", "in conclusion" or "let med end this by saying…" to tell signal closure. You can also change your pitch or the rhythm of your voice to show that the speech is ending. After doing so, you can finish the speech. Keep it short but do not end it up too quickly.

Do a Review

As you near the end of your speech, you need to restate your key points, the topic and the purpose. Have you tackled them all properly? Is everything clear to your audience?

Try to go back and discuss the key points, the topic and the purpose one at a time. You can ask your audience for feedback.

Let them tell you what they have learned from you. This is also the time to answer some questions that your audience might have.

Leave Something with the Audience

A good speaker does not simply talk in front of an audience and then leave afterwards.

A good speaker instills something in his or her audience – a new knowledge, skill or value that remains with the listener for a long time.

A speaker's main purpose is to motivate, inspire, and move people.

Challenge the audience to apply what they have learned from you in their day-to-day lives. Motivate them to create a change and go for something new.

Let your message linger with your audience for a long period and not just a brief moment.

To do this, you can still make use of quotations, questions, humor and stories. Make your speech memorable to your audience as much as you can.

CHAPTER 6

Proper Use of Language

Choosing the Right Words in Public Speaking

When doing a public speech, you should be able to properly convey your message and let everyone know what your thoughts are exactly.

To do this, you should learn to use language and words effectively. This will help the audience understand you and remember your message better.

Here are a few ways to enrich your vocabulary and help you covey more concise messages:

7. Read

   Obviously, the best way to widen your vocabulary is to read. Almost all successful speakers are also successful readers.

   Aside from widening your vocabulary, reading can also give you new knowledge. Try to read several pages of a book every day.

   You will start to see an improvement in your vocabulary and you will also be able to acquire new and valuable information.

2. Listen

   Another way to learn new words is by listening. You can listen to other people while they are talking and you may be able to hear an unfamiliar word.

Put the new words you hear on a list and look for their definition afterward.

You can attend seminars, conferences and gatherings and also learn new words there. Attending these sorts of things may also help you improve your speaking skills.

3. Learn a New Word Each Day

Try to learn a new word each day. Little by little, you will add new words to your vocabulary and before you know it you have learned a lot of interesting words.

You can go online to different websites or download applications to help you throughout your learning.

If you are a busy person, learning a new word each day is a great way to enrich your vocabulary without experiencing too much hassle.

CHAPTER 7

Speech Delivery

The Moment of Truth

The actual delivery of the speech is your moment to shine. For some this part is the most stressing part of delivering a speech.

This is the real thing. After making your draft and practicing speaking for a couple of times, this is the moment of truth.

In this part, it is most important to keep your calm and focus on what you are about to do.

Effective Delivery

For you to be able to effectively deliver your speech, you need to look natural in front of your audience. Avoid being too stiff or being too shaky. For you to be more natural and confident you must:

1. Act Normal

   You should keep in mind that your speech is just like any other normal conversation that you can have with any other normal person.

   A speech is only a little different because many people are listening to you all at the same time.

   However, you don't have to be nervous about this. Just think of everyone as your friend. Smile and be confident. If you are well prepared, there is nothing to be nervous about.

You can just imagine everyone in their underwear. If this old trick works for you, then go for it. Don't try to act it out. Try to keep everything as normal as you can.

2. Be enthusiastic

    Even if you are the one speaking, you need to show some enthusiasm over you topic.

    If your listeners see that you are excited about speaking, then they might be excited too.

    This will spark some interest in your audience and will help you keep their attention for a longer span of time.

3. Be confident

    Don't think too much about how you look, instead focus on what you are saying.

    Don't be too conscious of yourself in front of your audience. It will only increase your nervousness.

    If you are not confident yourself, how will your audience have confidence in you and in what you are saying?

4. Maintain Proper Contact

    When speaking, do not avoid the audience. What you should do is engage with them. Remember to maintain eye contact with everyone.

    Shift your focus from one person to another to see if everybody is listening. Maintaining your focus on only one person may cause him or her to be uncomfortable.

    However, if you just stare into blank space, your audience may not find your speech exciting or interesting. Also try to use a friendly tone of voice. Don't talk to loud or shout.

    You just need your voice to be heard clearly. You may raise your voice when pointing out to a fact or to an important idea.

But throughout your speech, you should try to talk in a calm and friendly manner. Also, don't forget to smile.

Remember to smile when you can and smile at the audience. If possible, put yourself in a place near your audience. This will create familiarity and a comfortable air around you.

Methods of Delivery

You can deliver your speech in many ways. As a speaker, you need to be familiar with the different methods of speaking.

But soon enough you can try to develop your own style and approach to speaking. Here are the most common types of delivering a speech…

1. Manuscript

   Speaking with a manuscript is the easiest way to do a public speech. You just need to read a prepared speech and hope that everything goes well. Most people do this type of delivery.

   However, this restricts you from maintaining eye contact with your audience, which is a must.

   You still can try to have a brief eye contact as you read, but much of your focus is on the paper that you are reading.

   This also restricts you from moving your body to show a point or portray conviction.

   As much of your attention is on the paper you are reading, you don't have much freedom to move and express yourself.

   This type of delivery, although easy, may be boring for the audience. Soon enough, their attention will drift away from you and you will have a hard time getting it back.

However, there are ways where you can still deliver an effective speech while reading a manuscript.

With enough experience and practice, you can speak in front of an audience without them getting bored, even while reading from a manuscript.

If you are about to read your speech, here are a few things you need to do:

o Use presentation aids to keep the attention of your audience.
o Take some time to read the whole speech and be familiar with it. This will help you avoid stuttering and making mistakes.
o It will also allow you to have some eye contact with your listeners.
o Use a font style that you are familiar with and try to put large spaces between each line of your manuscript. This will allow you to read it with ease and avoid misunderstanding words or phrases.

2. Memory

Delivering your speech from memory is a hard thing to do. First of all, if your speech is long, it would be hard to memorize it all.

Second, sometimes, when doing the actual speech you may forget something important and you end up confusing your audience.

However, delivering a speech from your memory may make you appear more professional.

If you can do it properly, it means that you took time making your speech and that you know the important details that need to discuss.

Of course, sometimes, you really can't help but forget something, so it is important to make an outline.

If you have memorized your speech, you can bring this outline with you while you talk. Sure, it does not contain your whole speech, but it has the key points and ideas you want to talk about.

But if you are still a bit unsure, you can bring with you your manuscript. Just take quick glances when you forget something.

There are still instances when memorized speeches are used. Speeches like this are common in toasts and introductions where you only need to say few short sentences.

Delivering a speech from memory has a few advantages:

o   You can maintain eye contact with your audience if you deliver your speech from memory and analyze how they think or react to your speech.
o   Maintaining eye contact is important for you to keep a certain bond or connection with your audience.
o   You can move around freely. Without a piece of paper consuming your focus, you now move around and interact with your audience. You can go around the stage and move your limbs freely. This will help you convey information more effectively.
o   You can express yourself more and vary the tone of your voice. You can smile, frown, or laugh when you have the most of your focus on your audience. Just like having the freedom of movement, this will also allow you to express your message more effectively.

3. Impromptu

Impromptu speaking is when you are not prepared to give a speech, which means that you need to improvise.

This can happen in many places, especially in celebrations, where you will be asked to do a little speech for someone.

This can also happen in school when your professor asks you to summarize a lesson from your book.

When speaking impromptu, you can be unprepared, but do not panic. There a things that you can do to ensure a good outcome for your speech.

- o Take a deep breath and focus on the situation. If you can, try to do a little bit of research first, but if you can't, just focus on what you know about the topic and on what you would really want to say to your audience.
- o On a piece of paper, write down key idea, phrases or topics that you would want to talk about. If you can, arrange them into a neat order and use a simple outline.
- o Stay focused on your topic. Do no wander off and try to talk about other things, get straight to the point and avoid too many words.
- o Don't speak too fast because your audience may not understand you. Instead, try to appear calm and speak slowly. This will allow you to gather your ideas while speaking.

Conclusion

Thank you again for downloading this book!

I hope this book was able to help you gain ideas on how to start public speaking as a beginner and helped you discover interesting new things.

The next step is to go out there, test your skills and enjoy!

Finally, if you enjoyed this book, then I'd like to ask you for a favor, would you be kind enough to leave a review for this book on Amazon? It'd be greatly appreciated!

Please leave a review for this book on Amazon!

Thank you and good luck!

www.ingramcontent.com/pod-product-compliance
Lightning Source LLC
Chambersburg PA
CBHW070924180526
45168CB00005B/2137